Dip it in

Written by Mollie Schofield

Collins

Tip it in.

Pam tips it.

Dip it in. Dan dips.

Sam dips. Pam dips.

Tap it.

a pan

Pat it.

Pat it, Sam.

Sam pats.

Dan taps.

Pam pats.

Dan dips in. Sam sips it.

a pad

a tin

🐾 Review: After reading 🐾

Use your assessment from hearing the children read to choose any GPCs and words that need additional practice.

Read 1: Decoding

- Ask the children to look at the following pages and mime each action as you read it, to check their understanding of the verbs:

  page 4: **Dip it**   page 6: **Tap it**   page 8: **Pat it**   page 12: **sips**

- Focus on the /p/ sound. Look at pages 14 and 15 together. Ask the children to take turns to find a word in the picture containing a /p/. Ask: Is the /p/ sound at the beginning of the word only or also somewhere else in the word? (e.g. *pineapple, peaches, pens, pencils, pen pot, plates, pears, penguin, pasta, potatoes, palm/plant, pepper pots, peppers, pads, pans*)

- Point to **Tap it** on page 6, allowing them to sound and blend out loud. Challenge the children to read page 7 but this time blending in their heads, silently, before reading the words aloud.

Read 2: Prosody

- Turn to pages 4 and 5, and model reading the text with expression, emphasising the action or the children's names.

- Ask children to take turns, reading page 4 or page 5, and experimenting with emphasising different words. Ask: What sounds best? Which words are the most important, and why?

Read 3: Comprehension

- Talk with the children about any cooking they have done. What did they make, and how? Can they mime some of the things they did? (e.g. *stirring, rolling*)

- Ask: What are the children making in this book? (*pizza*) How do you know? (*page 13 shows the finished pizzas*)

- Look at page 12 and ask: How did they make the pizzas? Prompt children by looking back at the pages:

  o pages 2 and 3, ask: What do they do first? (e.g. *tip water in and mix it*)

  o pages 8 and 9, ask: What are they doing now? (e.g. *checking/patting the dough*)

  o page 11, ask: What do you think they do after this? (*roll it out*) Prompt by showing the flattened bases on page 12.